AFTERMATH

ALSO BY SANDRA M. GILBERT

Acts of Attention: The Poems of D. H. Lawrence

In the Fourth World: Poems

The Summer Kitchen: Poems

Emily's Bread: Poems

Blood Pressure: Poems

Wrongful Death: A Memoir

Ghost Volcano: Poems

Kissing the Bread: New and Selected Poems, 1969–1999

Inventions of Farewell: A Book of Elegies (editor)

The Italian Collection: Poems of Heritage

Belongings: Poems

Death's Door: Modern Dying and the Ways We Grieve

On Burning Ground: Thirty Years of Thinking About Poetry

Rereading Women: Thirty Years of Exploring Our Literary Tradition

The Madwoman in the Attic: The Woman Writer and the Nineteenth-Century Literary Imagination (with Susan Gubar)

No Man's Land: The Place of the Woman Writer in the Twentieth Century (in three volumes, with Susan Gubar)

Masterpiece Theatre: An Academic Melodrama (with Susan Gubar)

Shakespeare's Sisters: Feminist Essays on Women Poets (editor, with Susan Gubar)

The Norton Anthology of Literature by Women: The Traditions in English (editor, with Susan Gubar; three editions)

The House Is Made of Poetry: Essays on the Art of Ruth Stone (editor, with Wendy Barker)

MotherSongs: Poems for, by, and about Mothers (editor, with Susan Gubar and Diana O'Hehir)

Feminist Theory and Criticism: A Norton Reader (editor, with Susan Gubar)

AFTERMATH

Poems

Sandra M. Gilbert

W. W. NORTON & COMPANY

NEW YORK · LONDON

For information about permission to reproduce selections from this book,
write to Permissions, W. W. Norton & Company, Inc.,
500 Fifth Avenue, New York, NY 10110

For information about special discounts for bulk purchases, please contact
W. W. Norton Special Sales at specialsales@wwnorton.com or 800-233-4830

Manufacturing by Courier Westford
Book design by Ellen Cipriano
Production manager: Devon Zahn

Library of Congress Cataloging-in-Publication Data

Gilbert, Sandra M.
Aftermath : poems / Sandra M. Gilbert. — 1st ed.
     p. cm.
ISBN 978-0-393-08112-1 (hardcover)
1. Grief—Poetry. 2. Loss (Psychology)—Poetry.
I. Title.
PS3557.I34227A69 2011
811'.54—dc22
                              2011007715

W. W. Norton & Company, Inc.
500 Fifth Avenue, New York, N.Y. 10110
www.wwnorton.com

W. W. Norton & Company Ltd.
Castle House, 75/76 Wells Street, London W1T 3QT

1 2 3 4 5 6 7 8 9 0

IN MEMORY OF DAVID GALE

CONTENTS

ACKNOWLEDGMENTS   13

I. OLD RECIPES

October Sunlight, Place des Vosges, 4:45 PM   17
Old Recipes   19
   O where are the long-gone picnic-perfect days   19
   Where's southern Bob, who turned a wicked
      phrase   20
   Where are the kids who tumbled through
      my house   21
   Where are the Hallowe'ens & Christmases   22
   Where's *What*, who boiled up this starry mess   23
Crochet Hook   24
"A Sundowner"   25
For Ilinca   28
"When my mother dies"   29
How we didn't tell her   30
His sorrow   33
The Lost One   35

Cremation, September 23, 2009   37

Grief: A History   39

March 13, 2004: Sunset View   43

The Anniversary   45

Anti-sonnet   46

December 1, 1957   47

Moving Out   49

After eighteen years   51

II.   PLANE

Earthquake Weather   55

Plane   57

Nature & Culture   58

The night mare   60

Question and Answer   62

    Holocausts   62

    At least   63

Portal = Portal   64

Labor Day   66

Nothing nicer   67

Materia Medica   68

    MRI Sonnet   68

    Colonoscopy Sonnet   69

    Contact Lens Sonnet   70

    Bypass Sonnet   71

    Dental Sonnet   72

    Cataract Surgery Sonnet   73

    Tooth Implant Sonnet   74

    Arthritis Sonnet   75

III. AFTERMATH

AfterMath   79
   Triple A   79
   Grapefruit   80
   Machine   81
   Eyes   82
   Surgery   83
   Continuous Passive Motion after Total Knee
     Replacement   84
   Bequest   85
   Shirts   86
   Cardigan   87
   Kite   88
Hospitality Cart   89
I'm shrinking, you said   92
Enormous vines   94
Map   95
Why?   97
Oysters Rockefeller   98
St. Joseph's, San Jose: March 4, 2009   100
Scouring   103
Fibonacci Sonnet   105

IV. DRASH

Drash   109
Paysage Moralisé   111
Whose transgression left the dead   112
November Coast   114
What's there   115

9

Edge of Winter Sonnet   116

Variations on an Old Issue of *Woman's Day*   117

   January 15, 1991, Only $1.09   117

   Be Safe in a Recession   117

   When Cheaper Is Better—28 Ideas   118

   7 Money Mistakes to Avoid   118

   How to Survive a Crisis   119

   Doctor's Tips for Younger Skin   119

   Free 1991 Bible Calendar   119

   Mary Ellen's Household Hints to Help

     the Earth   120

   Give Yourself the Best Body of Your Life:

     Easy Diet and Workout Plan   121

   Contest! Win a $15,000 Bedroom   121

   How to Keep Your Kids Well This Winter   122

   The Problem People Won't Admit: Like 28

     million other Americans you might have a

     serious hearing problem—and not even know it.

     Don't suffer in silence! See page 32.   122

   Meat Meals to Fix in Minutes   123

Holy Saturday & nothing   125

Sun in Fog   126

Said the scribe   127

V. LEI SOUP

   The Same Ground   131

   Seeds   133

   The Zugspitze/Pike's Peak   134

Parasailor   136
   Fiesta siesta on the breezy beach   136
   The bounce of clouds among the Mary blues   137
Seal Viewing Point: Disturbance of Sea Mammals
   Is a Federal Offense   138
Mother and Child   139
Flocks   141
The Berkeley Rat   142
The Paris Mouse   144
He's   146
For Ruth Stone on Her Ninetieth Birthday   148
Fourteen Fourteeners for Sophia at 14 Months   149
Anti-Valentine   150
Canticle of the plums   151
Calla lily, shameless   152
Hearing Aids   153
   Hugging   153
   Sex Sounds   154
   Later   155
   Morning   156
   What does he hear?   157
Lei Soup   159
Knowing   160

ACKNOWLEDGMENTS

Agenda: "Parasailor," "Seeds"

Alhambra Poetry Calendar: "The Berkeley Rat," "The Paris Mouse" (reprint)

Babylon Burning/nth Position: "Portal = Portal"

DMQ Review: "Grief: A History," "The night mare," "Sun in Fog," "Mother and Child," "Flocks" (featured poet)

Green Mountains Review: "Calla lily, shameless," "Hospitality Cart," "Said the scribe," "For Ruth Stone on Her Ninetieth Birthday" (reprint)

InterReview: "Variations on an Old Issue of *Woman's Day*," "Knowing"

Michigan Quarterly Review: "Question and Answer," "Contact Lens Sonnet," "Dental Sonnet"

Natural Bridge: "For Ruth Stone on Her Ninetieth Birthday"

Poet Lore: "What's there," "The Same Ground," "Anti-Valentine"

Poetry: "The Paris Mouse," "Colonoscopy Sonnet"

Poetry International: "March 13, 2004: Sunset View," "The Anniversary," "Earthquake Weather"

Smartish Pace: "October Sunlight, Place des Vosges, 4:45 PM"
  "Lei Soup"
Solo Café: "The Zugspitze/Pike's Peak"
Southwest Review: "How we didn't tell her"
TriQuarterly: "Old Recipes," "AfterMath"
2 Bridges Review: "MRI Sonnet," "Tooth Implant Sonnet,"
  "Bypass Sonnet," "Fibonacci Sonnet"

I'm grateful for the illuminating discussions I've had with various members of my Berkeley poetry circle—among them, Dan Bellm, Chana Bloch, Jeanne Foster, Dorothy Gilbert, Diana O'Hehir, Peter Dale Scott, Phyllis Stowell, Mark Turpin, Alan Williamson, and Anne Winters. In addition, I thank my editor, Jill Bialosky, along with my agent, Ellen Levine, for their continual support, and David Stanford Burr for lively and meticulous copyediting.

I.

OLD RECIPES

October Sunlight,
Place des Vosges, 4:45 pm

How could I not
in this great light
the chestnuts slowly bronzing—

music indistinct along the walks
under the echoey arcades—
clear water in the fountains rising

falling streaming glittering—
& babies bubbling out of strollers or
scooping sands in jolly pails—

& bodies indistinctly flung
on plates of grass
or moving through light

& shadow on the hard-packed leaf-strewn
paths among the green—
how could I (but I could)

not think of my dead—
their faces quickly withering
& blown along these roads

around the Place
where centuries have stood
in this same afterglow of summer

listening to children's cries
& peering toward a blue that still
recurs through tents

of leaves still
yellow green
& circled by the rose & white

old stone of those old palaces
how could I
(but I could)

not bear to think

Old Recipes

O where are the long-gone picnic-perfect days

when we reeled a sunny woozy loop from house
to house, broad Effie, red-faced Bob, with bowls
of eggplant soup, grilled *crépinettes*, wild rice,
Moneera with vine leaves, Myrna with garlic snails—
then down to the clammy beach, where Bob and Doug
snuggled under a cliff & cavorting kids
kicked sand while my mom, throned on a splintery log,
lamented loneliness & passed out Band-Aids.

Once "Uncle Fred" led our children over the bluff
& down to—*where?*—while I clutched their daddy's wrist
in terror—then they marched back looking tough
(& unapologetic Fred came last)—

O those were Fellini days of *dolce vita*,
when the glass was full, the margaritas sweeter!

Where's southern Bob, who turned a wicked phrase

while stirring negronis that were stronger, sweeter,
than what you could drink at Harry's Bar in Venice?
Where are his steaming pots of *rebollito*,
his lazy days on the sofa watching tennis?
Where's Doug, who stole Bob's heart & then his house?
And what of Moneera, who was stout & stern
till cancer gobbled Bob's esophagus
so *she* couldn't eat or sleep, her pounds were gone. . . .

Now Doug is sunk under the water table,
Moneera stumbles & trips across her cane,
Bob's seersuckers have gone to the Goodwill,
and we'll never eat his Hoppin' John again,

but the bygone days were lucky with casseroles,
charades & lyrical imbroglios.

Where are the kids who tumbled through my house,

their sidewalk hopscotch, teen imbroglios,
the kitchen glasses crashing ("it just broke"),
the lunchbox Ding Dongs, the SpaghettiOs,
the candles flaring on the birthday cake?
And where's their dad, who once, when left alone,
roasted & stuffed a turkey for himself,
and boiled the carcass, strained the leavings fine—
where's his broth, his bark, his bite, his laugh?

Driving past flocks on the greening hills, he joked
"Little lamb who made thee," then replied,
"Brillat-Savarin made me!" Born to be cooked,
the snowy babies innocently baaed.

They didn't know they'd be chopped up & browned,
or end (like him) in an oven underground.

Where are the Hallowe'ens & Christmases,

those special days on cosy sacred ground?
Like ninepins lined along the festal board,
grandma, grandpa, mom, dad, aunties dined—
lobster salad, eggplant caviar!—
with treats for kiddies heaped on the buffet
or a tinselly tree aglow in the living room.
Sometimes we'd been to midnight mass to pray,
but still the ninepins toppled one by one.

Then came the priests with holy bread & wine,
and magic oil to seal God's pact with us:
their purple swallowed grandma & her cane,
grandpa *et al.* all fell into their chalice,

and now the long-gone children's holidays
glimmer & fade in ghostly videos.

Where's What, *who boiled up this starry mess,*

this ache of dread that haunts the videos
and tightens like one nerve along the food chain?
Suppose it's all just tooth & claw, suppose
zero times zero roasts in the toasty oven?
Blue saints & pasty abbesses once planned
al fresco luncheon dates in paradise,
and Hindu fakirs sat on nails & thinned
while Buddha gained weight awaiting emptiness.

What sweets for the sweaty, though, the fleshy mob
hungering for picnics in the grass?
Spread out the blanket, love, unpack your bib,
wipe that sneer away & raise a glass

to the yeasty nothing that makes the cupcakes rise,
and the nothing that fattens the picnic-perfect days.

CROCHET HOOK

Because she couldn't knit she just crocheted,
alone with Johnny Carson, night after night.
(Those jokes screened out the news that terrified
quakes and crashes and muggings in the street. . . .)
So the dark vests grew in endless simple loops
as the onscreen shadows chattered, the band blared,
and the room filled up with odd familiar shapes
and she hooked and slipped to show she wasn't scared
when the "icebox" wheezed as if it were alive
or the radiators clanged their cryptic code
and the pilot ticked its answer from the stove,
    until at last she drowsed in her solitude
      and the fallen yarn pooled at her feet like blood.

"A Sundowner"

is what the doctor said
my ninety-seven-year-old mother
screaming and cursing

and kicking suffered
two days ago in the hospital
where she was taken after

falling and breaking
two ribs in the bathroom
of the "assisted living facility"

that I forced her into
just last summer
once she started fighting

with her imaginary "visitors,"
the "cotenants," so she claimed,
who maybe came because she'd lived

so long with shadow in that sad, gray-
shadowed rent-controlled New York
apartment that the shadows

thickened into flesh,
became women cooking at a magic
stove behind the bookcase,

mothers nursing babies under my dead
father's desk, lovers coupling
in a secret shade

beneath the rose-silk-covered *pouf*
my parents bought before
they even dreamed of me:

and when it's dark, the doctor
said, "old folks in every ward
get stressed, confused and scared,

disoriented, this is very common"—
as common as not wanting
other urgent lovers

under her rose-silk *pouf,* as common as
saying, pleadingly,
the way she did in "assisted living,"

just a day or two
before her fall, before
her sundown in the hospital,

"Listen, Sandra,
I'm still too young
to be shelved like this."

For Ilinca

Why should I even worry, dearest Ilinca,
about how & what I did at the poetry reading,
what is poetry, how can I even think
of meter, metaphor, as you lie dying,
swollen & agonized in your pretty gown,
the IV dripping, the hired practical nurse
poised by the hospital bed in your living room—
and what's the use of language, what is verse
when I think of your beautiful face, your yellow hair,
your long pale body stilling and lapsing out,
out into dirt & grass & nothing more:
you'll never love again—or bleed—or eat,
    dearest Ilinca, & I tell you in a sonnet
    as certain as if I bet my whole life on it.

"WHEN MY MOTHER DIES

I'm going to go to Denmark,"
she said cheerfully.
Said brightly.

We sat at the California wedding feast,
chicken bones on our plates.
"How," I began. . . .

The little wrinkled cancer-riddled Danish
mother lay at home,
reading, and wheezing now and then.

We mopped our plates with crusts of bread.
The bride and groom were cutting
into the first thick layer of cake.

In Jutland foxes barked among the hills.
The daughter wore silky red and black,
and on the misty island of Fanø,

where the mother was born,
the tall waves of the North Sea
broke and broke.

How we didn't tell her

that the housekeeper said that
the gardener said that
someone named

Jean or Jeannie or Jenny
who was his friend or maybe
his boss had said that

today that just
today he was hit by a car
& he was killed he died

at once in the prime
of his handsome youth he
who was her youngest her

onetime baby ice-cream
cone with dimpled arms
& scrumptious tummy he

who gardened & prayed
for purity on earth
but we said let's wait let's

wait to tell her till we're
sure & we called the gardener
the housekeeper the irrigation lady

the police the coroner
the highway patrol the neighbors
we called everyone but her

until at last the gardener
said no no how could the housekeeper
get it so wrong it wasn't

him it was someone else who was
hit by a car & killed
today & we rejoiced & were

glad we hadn't told her because
his handsome flesh his pulsing
prime returned to us as a gift

more precious than before
& as for the other one, the other
mother's son who really died

today we let him go we
didn't give him
another thought.

—FOR CHANA & JONATHAN

His sorrow

masters his sleep:
nightly he's unmanned—
& yet so manly that his grief

cries out her name in a deep
voice bearded with the weird
testosterone of pain.

How can my hands
comfort him, my
loneliness

naked after the torn
sleeves of my own shivah, the ripped
seams I can never mend?

He wants her to come back
from that bad
speechless glare,

the searing crystal of the place
where she turned
into a pillar that wouldn't

ever turn toward him again,
though she'd still love him
if love could live

in a heart of salt.

The Lost One

Far beyond the breakers—
those violent white scribbles—& far
beyond the indifferent

moat of the fog
& infinitely smaller than the pebbles
of starlight the telescopes

don't pick up,
she rides the sky he wants
to dream:

size 4 suit, tight
coiffure, serious glasses,
masterful, sober,

reading her portion
of the night: the fate
he'll never forget.

You, poet, watch his dreams,
you aren't in them but you
write them down,

& you write *that* down too.
And the breakers
speak their snarl of sentences

while great fish pace beneath
the glimmering surface,
& hawks loop above the pines

at the edge of the beach.

CREMATION, SEPTEMBER 23, 2009

The box, the long gray flimsy box,
a box for a tall bouquet, a delivery
box, a box of body,

of face, of flickering
changes of face,
of "once there was"

& "now there's me"
poised at the sill
of awe: a silent

roaring that just goes on
& on, a gray door
that slowly rises

& a wrenching begins,
something
turns a weighty handle

& now the body that has forgotten
its box of words,
slides with its

tongue of a shrunken leaf, its
useless eyelids,
along a brief

slick track
into a mouth of flames
that are never still,

yet never the same.

—IN MEMORY OF NANCY BASMAJIAN

GRIEF: A HISTORY

When you spun away in the whirlwind
my grief followed you
a whimpering spaniel

you were gone your absence
was absolute & my grief
sat on my kitchen table
a vase of bloody roses

my grief sprang from my breastbone
a young birch swaying & scabrous

my grief was a dull pot
at the back of the stove

my grief lashed the windows
a hurricane with your face

my grief sulked & silenced itself
a fog over the harbor

my grief in tatters
my grief in gusts
my grief skulking around the house
ready to kill

and behind it alongside it
ahead of it
in their march of plenitude
the five musicians came

one at the far left drumming
on old stones with hands
like heavy gloves
and one on the far right
with a steely mandolin displaying
ecstasies of syncopation

and one just left of center scraping
a violin whose pure implorings
shone above the road

            & one
just right of center
pulsing lunatic heartbeats

& in the midst
the dark the stout
accordionist came staggering & falling

under the weight of his keyboard
with its trills & trickles
its hundred pipes

its massive lurching chords
that led them on all five
as they tramped the dust

as they flung ahead through
the whirlwind where you hide

as they stomped on my glitter
of grief my shards of
rage

      & scraps of children
shrieking with joy
followed swift as swirls of paper

& I too I followed
until there we were
where we hadn't been:

& it was moonrise down on the riverbank
& the pipes at the center piped lower
like shadow pipes

oh there by the muddy river
where the waters unfold
& flow in their helplessness

the last pipes piped
their solitude of grief

March 13, 2004: Sunset View

At the first light of spring, I bring you narcissi,
their delicate pale heads drooping, drugged
with the breath of their own perfume.

How clear your stone is after all this time,
more than a decade since some unknown carver
was paid to drill your name in polished granite

& decades more since our youngest child was hurled
weeping into this same light of March.
Now your body that was once my body too

is nothing but a rag for spiders spinning
their own histories. What news do you have
for us? And what can we say to you that *means*?

Our youngest isn't happy, & the light of spring
casts a chill on the cut narcissi
that I flung across the stone

where your name still burns an eerie white
as if you could rise between its bars, above
the wilted flowers, the deepening marks that say

I lie among shadows with another man,
she lies alone with hope & dread——& you,
no longer you, you lie with the solemn spinning things

that move the light of March into its own decay.

—FOR E.L.G.

The Anniversary

mustn't be worded or worried any more
now that two cycles of seven have passed away
and moon by sun by week by quickening year
I too have passed past too much memory—
And whose was the anniversary anyway?
Was it hers who sobbed and put her head in the oven,
was it theirs who made this day their wedding day,
or his who couldn't keep from getting born?
The tumult of birth pummeled and plunged him out,
nothing could stop the clenched fist of the womb,
the lips that gaped and uttered him head to toe,
the *what* that made him ugly or smart or handsome—
    and then (as you lay dying) the afterbirth,
    the cage of breath, the blood, the aftermath.

—FOR E.L.G., FEBRUARY 11, 2005

Anti-sonnet

Fifteen years in the sweet-scented meadow, its grasses
restlessly balancing tendrils and tips of light,
and the ocean juggling the sky in bits and pieces,
and the cattails crinkling in the yellow heat. . . .
No, no more about the meadow, say
goodbye to the seasons, to pastorals, to dopey
moping sheep, to brooding sky and sea,
those teary tropes for sorrowful and sloppy!
Emily Brontë, Judith Wright, you both
already counted up the wild fifteen
when one's above, an other *cold in the earth:*
ghostly, you tell me to whistle a different tune—
give voice to the rock, find words for the bed of granite,
and don't describe tough stuff in another sonnet!

December 1, 1957

I was twenty. You were twenty-seven.
(It was your birthday.)
Our parents were fifty somethings
& the grandparents in their seventies.

Everybody wore hats.
We ate Cornish game hens stuffed with wild rice.
A string quartet played the waltzes from *Rosenkavalier.*
Cousins & fathers & brothers uttered toasts.

When we cut the cake, Monsieur Charles, the maître-d',
surprised you with a cupcake on which a single candle rode.
(I had arranged for that.)
There was white satin, as usual, & the usual rice.

We had three children, four grandchildren
—a little girl you never met is at this moment
crying in the next room, & the sun
is climbing over the cypresses.

As is customary, more than two thirds of the party
are now dead, including of course you,

and who will wave and smile
in the backseat of the car,

who will roll down the window
and let in the cold air?

—DECEMBER 1, 2007

Moving Out

Darling, I'm pushing the house
into the garden, into the black arms,
the green embrace
of the oaks. Yesterday,

two giants lugged the grand piano,
its synapses still crackling with your tunes,
up the steep steps, the narrow path
to the gate. Now it muses

in the *what is this* of a warehouse,
and the silence
where it used to stand
has forgotten your forte.

Out in back of the back,
workers dig in unsteady rock,
but now the house is moving
faster than they can hew and hack:

the house has started to unpack:
its walls possess new places,
doors flap open,
windows heave from hinges—

and now the sofas fly
into a maze of ivy,
the hallways gaping
under a hollow of sky!

Only the piano keys,
hidden under their ebony hood,
remember your touch,
and wait, and are still,

and brood.

After eighteen years,

the chiaroscuro of your absence
still splits the bloody
hearts of the blossoms,

so now, for the first time,
I light a Yahrzeit candle for you,
& stand it near the stove,

where it flickers against steel,
trying to call you back from stone,
trying to tell you

how you'd have loved
the little ones
playing games on

your grave last week—
their mops of difference,
red & blond & brown,

bent in concentration,
their small fists grabbing
& ratcheting the gears

that brighten the moving
puzzle they brought.

—FEBRUARY 11, 2009

II.

PLANE

EARTHQUAKE WEATHER

Twenty years ago I'd have written
earthquake weather:
a hard sun cracks the ground,
the sea draws back,

its nude anemones exposed,
and the black claws of the cypresses
dig into the cliff
for dear life.

O all the phenomenal world
thickened with omens then—
the dead fish on the beach, the motherless
seal in the windbreak. . . .

And now—O now, dear life,
I tiptoe to the edge, peer over
the foam that slides away,
the sticks and bones cast off,

while overhead a hawk
stands on a blue hill of air,

staring down too,
to where in the motionless

heat two bulldozers
flatten the next field.

Plane

Some are sleeping very darkly in tight places
as if they no longer know or need to know
how this long vibration

is taking them   Some
are looking at flat or folding things
puzzling over lines   squinting at images

Some are prowling the narrow passageways
or limping or staggering
& now & then there are openings

where others in uniforms
emerge with trays & papers from spaces
with closets of ice   cupboards

of tools   & over all
the humming of something that grinds
hisses   throbs   goes on

& on through what is
all at the same time
huge   tiny   shining

blank   misty

Nature & Culture

The heaviness
of the August chestnuts
in the Place des Vosges

their nuts like prickly pears
that stick & prickle
among vast flat-headed downward-turning

tiers of leaves
the green
inside the flat vast leaves

the houses straight & duly
pink around the royal
square the king decreed

diagonals of light
inside the square
& circles

of swallows swooping
& children skipping
& the drunken

sans-abri under the arches
(the *sans-abri* who will
freeze to death next winter)

& the what inside the green
the bland inside the sky
the bland impassive sky

inside the houses

The night mare

comes up from the field, her
nostrils twitching, her
hide jumping with fleas.

She's white against black grass—
a spasm under the trees,
her hooves hearts knocking.

Old shape-shifting clop-clopper:
she carries you from the lake
to the pit where

you build the chapel
of panic, & she's the mice
chattering inside the organ, the angel

who lets drop the window
of heaven that shatters
next to the altar,

         & under
a quilt of shadows she's
the thin one

who enters the pulpit & asks
how can you praise God
after the soldiers made the eyeless rabbi

dance naked in the marketplace.

Question and Answer

Holocausts

of bullets in Haditha, so they say
another My Lai, another Babi Yar,
another corner of another grisly
"death event"—
               another slam of war
where "scale is reckoned" by "compression of time"
through which annihilation is "delivered"
to every baby, mama, papa, home—
field—street—that can be smashed and slivered.

Why wonder how babies squirmed or cried, mamas
cowered (sighting rifle-toting fellow
humans)—why think of families in pajamas
flailing, *dies irae, dies illa?*

Why defy Adorno, helpless poet?
Why struggle to name the bullets in a sonnet?

At least

attest what you've heard-not-seen of bone and skin
unzipped like the body bags they'll go in now,
and the kid who held his little sister's head in
shaky hands but couldn't—
                              it all fell through
(through wounds, through holes), *everything fell out*—

and it fell out too that the kid fell also,
falling like the smoke the bombs create
and decreate as fires bloom and blow.

O socko awe! O Mussolini's rose,
exploding rose of everywhere, what tests
you try us with, what trials no sentences,
no testimonies, equal.

                              And the ghosts
of bullets disappear in dirty mists,
of kids in puffs of dust, demented lists.

PORTAL = PORTAL

meli-
fluous fluent fluvial
saxo-
phone go on go
thickly thirstily
on on-
stage beyond the state
of war the theater
of blood the sky
exploding over Baghdad

he smiles alive
& kicking in the beat
beatitude
he lifts his left
foot &
paws the ground
the music tossing him
around until he's
nothing but a
weed on a thundering shore

& my curly-haired
faun-
eyed grandson tries
to hold his sax like that

the pan posture
the piper posture
with a sax in-
stead of a rifle &
instead of a poem
that pleads for peace

(the hardest kind to write
because why
should anyone
have to)

—FOR MICHEL PORTAL, SAXOPHONISTE
& VAL GILBERT, SAXOPHONIST

Labor Day

at the edge of the late summer
simmering field

sudden characters rear up,
each armed with tiny claws, each

bearing minute pink-purple cups
the color of raw flesh, the color

of pleasure scraped away
all summer long.

What comes after Works and Days?
In no time the flesh-flash of the thistle

goes white, goes airy and soulful.
Shall we spin toward Thanksgiving

forgetting everything,
even the dull thump of the sea?

NOTHING NICER

than being in the hospital, I
said to myself as I got off the phone
with my dear eighty-two-year-old friend who's

fading from heart failure
at a nearby institution:
there all is *luxe, calme et volupté,*

the nurses skimming in & out like gulls
in their jeans & sneakers & badges,
the doctors all pretending to care,

the potted plants, the candies, the puffed-up
flowers, the views:
sunsets flashing on wide glass

if you're on the right side of the building,
maybe dawn the other way—
& the long white blinds you can draw down

as evening thickens
& lights preen in the whispering
corridors, & you ask for more,

more heated blankets.

Materia Medica

MRI Sonnet

Archimedes, Galileo, Newton,
even Einstein—whaddya think of this?
A hail of tiny hammers, mini Vulcan,
flung at a single elderly meniscus!

Percussion symphony, the pounding makes
a pattern from what wants to talk, hug,
snuggle or scold; the pitter-patter takes
echo for granted, sounding out my leg
into a grosse fugue of knee & ankle
set in presto staccato tempi, tempi
that trace the flights of, Archimedes, smooth to wrinkle,
falls of, Galileo, swift to limpy. . . .

Noisier than the speed of light the measure,
O Einstein, of the vanishing of pleasure.

Colonoscopy Sonnet

On the news tonight, a presidential
colonoscopy—a tale of how
for three whole hours the chief exec of trouble
handed trouble to his vice (although
no double trouble came), but then no more
details revealed: no bacterial armies
multiplying in a flare of war
among kingly polyps & no kinky creases.

Welcome to the presidential gut,
bubble gum pink, not a spot of shit
(after a quick administrative cleanout)
where global decisions stir & sit in state,
    and the first physician's mighty pointer traces
    only microdrops of blood in secret places.

Contact Lens Sonnet

Strange how these little films of vision—shreds
of Saran wrap—grow when I paste them to
my eyes, sometimes veiling sight in shards
of itchiness, always huge & aglow
with continents of fabulous details:
angles edges insects wrinkles feathers
ribbons pavings ruffles pebbles petals
that disappear the minute I peel the layers
of sight away!
               O then I'm stuck in the fuzz
& fog of horizons my naked eyes supply,
misty gleanings of what might be, no *is*
to be sure of, nothing that wants to clarify—
  and I have to glue the tiny monsters back
  so "reality" can play its giant trick.

Bypass Sonnet

When they sawed you open & then laid bare
that little squirming animal your heart,
& the you that's you drifted into ether
while your wine-dark blood swirled away & apart
from the other you I also love—straight back,
fuzzy chest, shy sexual beard—
which one of the two you's did they dissect,
which did they restore to flesh & word?

You came back stunned & silent, swallowing hard,
like one who's passed by places where the cold
has claws that dip into throat & bone & blood.
You came back chilled, but then forgot the cold,
warmed up:
             the only sign of where you were
the passing line where they sewed you back together.

Dental Sonnet

What if millennia from now some grave
young archaeologist digs up a string
of yellowish teeth—stains, cavities,
incisors, molars, here & there a filling,
shrouded in such elemental dust
each single tooth might be a pebble torn
from the sweltering lava bed of history
that swaddles leaf & dinosaur & fern—

how will she clean each crevice, & will every
mottled edge disclose, for instance, how
the dentist in my ancient century
sprayed & scraped at these small stones,
                                    & how
with mouth agape I stared in the shining mirror
of that dispassionate gaze for half an hour?

Cataract Surgery Sonnet

As if I've merely seen through a glass darkly
all these years, as if a stream of shadow
drizzled through all hope of clarity
& bathed the world in a heavy rancid glow—
and oh, what power in those pools of gray,
weakening the sun, effacing me!
"Just routine cataracts," the doctors say,
& this one slides the lens from my left eye,
& substitutes a visionary blaze—
exploding staircases of light & shade! —
& the mirror's closeup judgment: a surprise
of lines I hadn't noticed, aging, speckled—
 a face I never thought I'd ever know,
  the one the looking glass makes you look through to.

Tooth Implant Sonnet

The head as furniture! A rounded board,
perhaps, that holds another board in place,
the headboard of an odd old-fashioned bed
on which the soul unrolls its lumpy mattress?
Under a dental glare, I'm the creaking head
of an old bedstead, & now some carpenter
drives in a screw so hard the tired wood
aches, groans, screams, begins to sliver. . . .

But would anyone clap a rubber mask over
the head of a bed, or pump in laughing gas?
The sober soul sneers at the metaphor,
& after all the head is stuffed with softness:
    a pillow, not a board? So what's-his-name
    finishes up with one last stitch in time.

Arthritis Sonnet

Am I stiffening into a rock of my fleshly self,
hunching through days, a person-shaped boulder,
old witch-statue on a kitchen shelf
peering down at the glowing muttering burner?
Too extravagant! After all, I'm half
titanium now, secret metals work
my hips & knee, midnight potions salve
my stony knots & knobs: but oh, don't look!
The mountain lion is fluent in his bones.
Last night he streamed along this road, a blur
of fur & tooth flashing past our gardens,
aimed at the tender fawn grazing under
the cliff that's shaped like your dead face, the one
when you were flesh you called by your own name.

—WALKING PAST THE ELLIOT ROCK AT THE SEA RANCH

III.

AFTERMATH

AfterMath

—FOR D.G., MATHEMATICIAN: D. 3/7/08

(Triple A)

He stood at the door, apologetic grin.
Morning on the street. Prebreakfast calm.
"Flat tire," he said. She barely glanced at him.
"Call Triple A." "I know," he said. "I'll call."
The last exchange; she turned to brew some coffee.
The big truck came in minutes, did the job.
Flat tire: they wrenched the wounded thing away,
replaced it, stored it, tinkered with the hub.

Ink of the *Times* soaking up the silence—
an ordinary, edge-of-springtime quiet.
No more words for now. Beyond the fence,
tulips & autos fractioning the light.

(Later the other engine, shiny and smart,
the one that tried but hardly fixed his heart.)

(Grapefruit)

He loved the taut, the pale-green geometric
segments, loved the cold matutinal
dissection, slicing/piercing the sour slick
of wedges (each an almost triangle):
every breakfast, then, a proof of calm,
the pleasure that repeats itself, the dear
quotidian, its fruitful tedium
perpetually there to think & master!

How did—how do—the lovely daily tastes
evaporate so fast? A "dizziness"
came rolling in & up in waves & twists,
a weird confusion, maybe a quick darkness. . . .
"It's coming again!" He choked & bit his tongue,
the tiny puzzle of the grapefruit gone.

(Machine)

On Friday at nine they came to "do the death."
His wondering mind, master of x & y,
stalled behind a veil of useless breath.

Did they unplug the lemmas, points, & pi?

Or did the great constants haunt him in the dark,
the primes on their endless luminous parade
swirling through blocs of meaning like a flock
of weighty gulls, each aglow with pride?

"They say he can hear you," someone warned, & so
she played intervals of noise to wake him up—
Schubert, Coltrane, & Bach, *fortissimo*—

though he lay sweating, ventilator off,

his only sound the strident rasping sigh
a body utters when it has to die.

(Eyes)

"Didn't they tell you? The hospice booklet says so—
three last expirations, then the eyes. . . ."
Crouched by the bedside, what could she hope to see—
what know—of how the discarded body does?

His breath came slower, loud, & even weird
as if from some fantastic faraway,
(the others huddled in corners, urgent, scared,
someone weeping, someone trying to pray)—

and then, with silence broadening into shock,
into a long astonishment of *still*,
the opening, like a struggle to awake
while diving backward into a deep pool:

his blue-gray eyes, circled with parchment white,
slowly widening; innocent; absolute.

(Surgery)

Musing on other tribes, Don't some, she asks,
mourn among rocks—fiercer than sitting *shivah*,
bleaker than the sympathetic masks,
stiff smiles & notebooks of the modern griever?
Can she flee to a pallor of her own, undo
the *nots* that sicken in a sorry self?
Can any smash of surgery renew
a measure of this stupid mournful stuff?

She dreams the OR, with its chilly din,
its ceiling Muzak, doctors, nurses, tool kits:
she dreams a cave of change that she can lie in,
flat & forgetful under swooping lights
while someone probes & opens & removes
the solemn thing that hurts, that weeps, that loves.

(Continuous Passive Motion after Total Knee Replacement)

She puts the aching leg in the magic shell,
goes blank: now curve or straighten, buckle, press
the little button—*then* lie still, big doll,
let the *power* begin to bend & flex & hiss!
On & up it goes, & on, around to nowhere—
heavy heaving thing on the empty bed,
heavily journeying in heavy air
away from what the other body did.

Past is replaced by part: the bloody flesh
will soon be hardened, rods of metal sealed
against untender bone: go on, great rush
of currents, hiss & flex & press & hold
her new tough body in this strange contortion
that might, or might not, be described as motion.

(Bequest)

She broods on the apartment back in the Marais,
the place where he wooed her, won her, where they lived
five months a year in eighty *mètres carré*
among rugs, songs, books they bought & loved.
Now *rien du tout*, her bequest nothing more
than dailiness—the table where he sat,
the yellow pads, the integers—no floor,
no walls, no three-dimensional estate.

Was she merely mistress, & mistress of nothing real,
chatelaine of phantom solids, zero keys?

Or was there a theorem in the fleeting whole,
a solution in that last of Paris days
when they hung the plate with the sultan's sigil on it
in happiness (as short-lived as a sonnet)?

(Shirts)

When there's nothing left to count or count on,
not a finger   whisper   breath   or gaze,
and she's locked in the elegant contraption
that bends her heavy legs—

> *flex! pause!*

pause! flex!—

> she thinks of counting:

> > *What?*

Well, then, just his shirts—the tattersall,
the plaid, the striped, the checkered red & white,
the heavy blue for winter, rust for fall. . . .

Whose shoulders will they hug, warm whose back
after waiting limp in the tangle of the closet
for just one man to come & look & pick?

—And flexing in her cloak of itch & sweat,
is she too waiting for some secret sum
of shirts, plus pause, plus silence—minus him?

(Cardigan)

"In his cardigan, dear God, his old red
lamb's wool L.L.Bean, the one I gave him
seven Christmases ago (or did
he order it himself, wanting *warm*
for winter, wanting cosy at his desk
to slide through theorems on the screen, or walk
the garden hunting pinecones in the dusk
& thinking Fibonacci—'nature's work,
so lovely and exact'!)
                              —the fine sad woollen
buttoned close, each sliver in its slot!

We left him in it on his bed, its woven
dark around his cold, his yellow-white,

—& did they take the cosy sweater off
or fire it up with all the other stuff?"

(Kite)

Watching from behind the chilly house
she sees it flash away, tumultuous skin,
fins in the air, triangles to use
the wind: wild geometry in motion.

Looping, quivering, sometimes almost crashing,
the flight itself's an argument for shape:
design tugs at the rope in the hand, the thrashing
tail's a lemma, propels the skyward leap.

But the thought is only paper after all,
a soul that clings to a stick, tears open, shreds
as it's flung to the ground in a final shiny fall,
and at last the line goes limp, the climbing ends.

Beyond the rush & sweep, an arc of silence—
though a mind imagined this flight, & proved it once.

Hospitality Cart

Yes we said *Yes that's okay*
yes we meant to take you off life support

so they brought a hospitality cart
laden with juices crullers coffee

warned us what we'd hear
("disturbing" stridor breathing)

took us into the white room where you lay
gasping though you didn't seem

to know you were gasping
or even that you were alive

& we stood around all ten of us
sipping juice & coffee

muttering half-remembered prayers
poems incantations

suctioning the blood that trickled
still

from the corners of your mouth
because you bit your tongue so hard

three days earlier when
to your surprise

your heartbeat stopped
(until the medics came)

stood there all ten of us
sipping & praying & watching

the warm movements of your
body in the morning sun

your body that would soon
be refined by fire

to a few pounds of grainy ash
your body several ounces

of which we flung today into the view
you loved at Cragmont Park

& divvied up the rest
in plastic baggies

your body that we inhaled
as the wind blew you

back to us   your
body that is now

dust on my bootsole
sorrow in my nostrils

your body that we keep on
portioning into smaller & smaller

packets some now tiny as
those little envelopes of sweetener

on the hospitality cart

I'm shrinking, you said,

so rueful, with that look of
wistful whimsy, cocking your head

a little to the side, as if
preparing to disappear altogether, or almost so,

like the Cheshire Cat, with just a smile of mild
surprise, & yes a bit of triumph:

There, I'll do it! What you never dreamed I'd do—
I'll enter the vegetable world & you'll have to after all

unplug me, or anyway uproot me,
like any other shriveled pumpkin or potato. . . .

And that smile, as you shrank!
After I'd forced you to get clipped—

when your hair was neat, your beard nearly *not* a beard—
the lines of your face were shrinking too, your face

was shrinking, narrowing, leaving
just your tender, rosy, full-lipped smile

as you slowly lost the fourth dimension
& the third, thinning to

lines I loved between
points of time I longed to hold—

& then in your darkened cardigan
you faded, slivered, became ashen,

yet were still a speck of brightness,
glowing *goodbye*,

from the shrunken city where they all go,
all the thinning ones

who suddenly slip between our fingers.

Enormous vines

began to sprout from the day you died,
dear love, dear
friend & protector,

& now they shade me, chill me,
tangle me in gross
darkness or weave

a thatch of cloud around me:
it's as if once more I walked
the dusky paths of the kiwi plantation

on the shore of that ice-black
lake in the mountains,
surrounded by lowering

branches like
arms of another species,
holding out sweet

suspicious fruit.

Map

My love, I opened
my dresser drawer this morning
& there was your heart

stored flat in glistening
film, slick black & white,
with all its enigmatic

shadows mapped by
the *Centre d'Imagerie Medicale Bastille*:
such a major guide we carried it

from continent to continent,
a talisman to keep our coupledom
intact (though just eight months ago

the three dimensions of your real
true heart
trembled & collapsed)—

yet here in grades of darkness
is a snapshot of what pumped you on
from plane to plane.

Darling, I left all the Michelins behind,
in our lost Marais,
with the Métro cards & cookbooks:

this black & white guide
to the narrowing pathways of your heart
is the only *Plan de Paris* I kept.

Why?

As we walked on the dusty ground of the event,
I said *why can't we try again?*

No, you said, & began somersaulting backward.

But it wasn't over, I said,
& over you went, over & over into

the land of backward, the mirror behind us.

O why, I said, *O why,*
don't you stop the invisible tears

of the child who weeps for you,

the dark-haired little one who yearns
in the vanishing mirror?

And you were silent, tumbling backward.

OYSTERS ROCKEFELLER

Frigid December twilight in Paris, hurrying
hungers, homeward bound, time

for a kir, for a Lillet, or even a whiskey
to ward off the cold, & you say you want

oysters Rockefeller, so we stop at the stand
for *crustacés* outside the Monoprix & buy

two dozen plump ones, & then at the *verger*
en face for the spinach, the parsley, the shallots,

& we have *gros sel,* a lot of it
to grill the hopeless little lumps of ocean

flesh alive, wrapped in a millionaire's
blanket of herbs—& O

the sweet salt green warm mouthfuls
of seaside innocence that we swallowed that night

slowly, tenderly, licking the shells & sipping
our *kirs* at our small round table,

each blessed taste of earth & ocean
still hot from a heavy bed of salt

itself so hot some devil might have
boiled down gallons & gallons

of the North Sea to leave this burning sparkle
of debris, just for us, just

for a few minutes in the icy
gut of winter.

St. Joseph's, San Jose: March 4, 2009

—IN MEMORY OF D.G.

There's no
candle to set aflame

in this strange church,
so dismal in the saintless

corners, rain stunning
the stains on the glass,

though the young priest
raises the symbols of this world

into what he prays is
the next—

       O sad wine,
be blood, O sorrowful bread,

be flesh, be
again for us.

O beloved dead ones
hovering

on the distant edges
of the possible,

weren't you possible
once, didn't you lift

your many-colored umbrellas
against a heaven

that opened just as today's
opens & lets down

water & light & darkness
in the afternoon?

The priest, in lenten purple, murmurs,
nods & beckons.

Amid shuffling of feet, damp
rustle of grown-up raincoats,

the children file forward
in their shiny windbreakers,

mouths open to receive
God's word. . . .

O Lord, why can't I walk toward you too,
hand in hand

with the shadows
who left me behind?

I would open my mouth
as those children do,

& pray, remembering
what that Danish physicist

remarked almost a century ago
about the lucky horseshoe:

They say it works
even if you don't believe in it.

Scouring

the oatmeal pot until it shines
like the salty waters of Loch Tuath

I think how I waited on the beach
one long ago late afternoon

as the tide slid toward me,
a sheet of white lace in the low sun.

You came with the two girls
over the fields, past shaggy startled

cattle & biting black flies
Through Kilninian Kirkyard, through

the rustle of oats & buckwheat
& other sacred grasses,

you came to the long pebbly beach
on that oddly sunlit western

shore of Mull
with its *shush* of salt & wind.

Now a stream of purifying water
pours over the breakfast pot.

And your mind now—is it too
brightened & scoured

of every last grain & seed?

Fibonacci Sonnet*

Dental chair, laughing gas, & now
fourteen months from your surprising death,
I summon Fibonacci, sage signor,
to ease my panic, calm & count my breath.
"Just a stick in the gums." "You *will* be kind of sore."
Zero plus one is one, plus two is three,
then five, then eight. "You'll feel a bit of pressure."
Thirteen, twenty-one. He rocks my jaw.
Plus thirty-four, then fifty-five.
                              You traced
these signs on pineapple, pinecone, sunflower.
Are they the lemmas of all life, all space?
My tooth heaves from its hole in my skull.
                                    I wonder

how Fibonacci's series would explain
why I still bleed when all your blood is gone.

* A sequence of numbers first created by Leonardo Fibonacci in 1202.
According to one commentator, it is "deceptively simple . . . but its
ramifications and applications are nearly limitless."

IV.

DRASH

Drash

*In the wilderness, in the wild place, in the tent of meeting,**
said the rabbi,

Yahweh spoke to Moses—
send forth of the tribe of Reuben: Eliẓur the son of Shedeur,

of Simeon, Shelumiel, the son of Zurishaddai,
and then that one, then these, then those:

the precise list of instructions
was nearly endless,

& His bellow
strained the seams of the tent,

the wind of His wishes
tore at the tired walls & roof,

ballooning them in & out like enormous lungs,
so even Moses, that master

of stuttering commands
cowered by the campfire,

* Numbers 1:1, 5, 6

& in the final, outer circle
the women & children whimpered.

Outside, under motionless starlight
the camels were restless, bridles

jangling as they cropped at whatever
there was to crop.

                    Tomorrow, again
the journey—the spinning sands,

the mirages of arrival
hovering over the great spaces

that must be crossed—although
that desert, like this one,

was in fact impossible to master,
despite the lurid

impatience of the Almighty.

Paysage Moralisé

Days and daze of light in the spidery
flecks of the thistle, the delicate
westward yearning
heads of the yellow grass,

and the sea so dark far out
under a tipped-over bowl of sunset!
I said to myself, *no sonnets, no paysages
moralisé*—but then

in the chill of the hollow
little pallid toadstools
lined the path like lamps arisen
from the underside of color,

and climbing into a last
minute of warmth I saw
the line of houses huddled
against an absence,

and heard the late birds
chip chip chipping
as if with miniature
hammers of steel.

Whose transgression left the dead

deer outside the hedgerow
three months ago
(a carcass from December, said

the mountain lion expert),
long white vulnerable
skull pointed toward

the safety of the cypresses,
skeleton whole and leather-
brown—its meat eaten by a thousand

mouths—elegant
spindly legs & ballet dancer
hooves ready to twirl

away from the tooth of the cougar
that must have punctured a tender
vein in the tense high neck. . . .

But what was
the gasp, the frantic
adrenaline in muscle

at the second of the kill,
what language for *Father*
why hast thou forsaken me

as life drained
into the flower bed,
staining the home of the purple

irises the gardener
tends each spring,
their stems locked safe in

sepulchral bulbs—
& though the expert says
the lion hunts a giant range

from hill to river to sea
dining at will
from May to December—

these now flourish
though they toil not,
neither do they flee.

November Coast

A great plateful of gray,
shifting its distances, its shivering
lid of air,

and draughts of white like the ones
decreed by Hermes Trismegistus—
as above so below—

in a changelessly changing
all-day dusk,
                    and now

the high grisaille
is spitting and spewing,
a scornful baby god,

and now it beams its rainbow
over the meadow,
                    and now the black

bristles of the hedgerow cypresses
score and scar a yellow glare
as the last light spreads its stain, and then

goes down, goes slowly down.

What's there

to write about but the daily
walk to the beach, the look at the sky, the seals,
the black mass of the cypresses, the rocks—

and even there, in the landscape,
what's to say?
A gust of nearly microscopic fruit flies

from the harvest down the road
fills the house with dancing *others* who
swim in my wine, skitter and skate

at the edge of everything:
why bother to write that down?
What else is new? What else is there to say?

Let go of this leaky pen is what I say.
Wipe your hands on your apron.
Stand in the doorway. Turn off the oven.

Regard the moon.

EDGE OF WINTER SONNET

New ice floes splitting the lake today,
jigsaw floaters each the white of *O*
so lonely for my youth in the liquid we,
the merge, the here-we're-all-together flow.
And the hard white sky talks back to them,
it says, *I see you now, you're each discrete,*
a fractured entity, the swaying sum
of cold and wind that cracks a whole apart. . . .

Another freeze, another metaphor
for winter's far too long-drawn-out largesse,
its strips of iron in the air, the sheer
pale amplitudes of ice we have to cross.

Can spring be far behind? You bet it can.
That mama underground won't give a sign!

—ITHACA, NEW YORK, MARCH 2007

Variations on an Old Issue of *Woman's Day*

1. January 15, 1991. Only $1.09

Sold at the checkout, with your
Trident, your razor blades.

Outside, the rain unfolds
its distances and pastel car hoods

melt like sno-cones
in the dazed half-light

of the half-empty parking lot.
On the black cover a blue

Dutch oven circles the ruddy
stew you think you want.

2. Be Safe in a Recession

Imagine the sun in Tehuantepec.
Imagine the frilled shields
of an ornamental January
cabbage flailing outward

like skirts of an upside-down
dancer. She's safe, though

receding, receding headfirst
into the pit of a redwood planter.

3. *When Cheaper Is Better—28 Ideas*

Attempt a lunar cycle.
Each day is an idea—viz,
Monday, Tuesday, Wednesday,
etcetera. If you can, ovulate.
Then menstruate. If you can't,
dream about what it might be like
if you could, or about what it was
like when you did.
Then try to find a moon—any moon—
and bleed. Pad yourself with catskins, dog
pelts, thorn lashes, root hairs.
And bleed.

4. *7 Money Mistakes to Avoid*

See above. Monday, Tuesday,
Wednesday, Thursday,

and etcetera.
Each named for a god you've forgotten.

5. How to Survive a Crisis

Simmer gently for as long
as necessary, as long

as you keep on wanting.

6. Doctor's Tips for Younger Skin

Imagine shadows.
Imagine shadows and coffins.
Touch the dreadfully soft

flattened leaves of the frozen
passion vine that lies in a
heap of itself

on your shimmering deck.
And get younger. You'll get
younger right away.

7. Free 1991 Bible Calendar

365 Wise Men marching
toward a moon, a star, a desert.

Staggering under signs that say
This time it's you we love.

Thor's day, Freya's day, Saturn's day
haunt them on the highway.

The atomic head of John the Baptist flares,
explodes, splotches the wallpaper.

8. Mary Ellen's Household Hints to Help the Earth

She recommends
S.O.S. and cleansing salt. But if
pressed she babbles
air, fire, water.

Dead leaves flip fretful
archaic pages
around her pointy shoes.
Her broom points north.

Get out your ironing board.
Put in a call to Tehuantepec.
Or a prayer to Freya.
Ovulate. Right away.

9. Give Yourself the Best Body of Your Life:
Easy Diet and Workout Plan

For example, admire the trivial
hairs of your arms. Thorn lashes, sperm
tails. Whipping in the wind.

And the great flat leaves
of the epidermis you call your own
and how they gather around a thin invisible core.

Think: I am and am not a body.

10. Contest! Win a $15,000 Bedroom

Forget about thistles and kitchens!
The long flat mattress
will be azure—*azul*—
to float on like a gull, scattering
cries of pride to those below, scattering

distances like rains of bad
dead leaves to those
who still stew under you.
And there'll be sheets of fire,
pillows of light.

But remember, you must fight for this.
The others are ardent, and the coins
will melt in your hands
the minute you draw them
from the aching oven.

11. How to Keep Your Kids Well This Winter

First, watch out for those distances
that hover like frozen leaves drifting

over the deck or thistle lashes
tempting a touch. Then maybe

you might try stories.
Tales of blue and mattresses or even

blood and stew are often
effective with children.

*12. The Problem People Won't Admit: Like 28 million other
Americans you might have a serious hearing problem—and not
even know it. Don't suffer in silence! See page 32.*

If you have to see page 32, probably
you aren't hearing right. Right?

So I'll write it down for you in plain
American black and white: if you

haven't read what I've said so far,
you'll go no further, you

with your swollen creamy youthful
hands, you with your serious

suffering in a silence
you can't even hear!

13. Meat Meals to Fix in Minutes

January 15, 1991. Only $1.09.
Won't you listen to the mushrooms
complaining, the meat

muttering that it's too late
for Mary Ellen, your body,
your bed? Your kids skid

through winter, your doctor tips
into easy blood, Jeremiah
moans—the madman!—as he marches

toward a March when the passion
vine might silently
resume its long crawl

up the walls of your house.
Light the oven. Fast.
Note this minute's

recession of darkness.
Avoid money mistakes.
Hurry up. Unfold

your flat pale leaves
like the skirts of a dancer.

Holy Saturday & nothing

happens—a stillness
of winter films

the grass, & the ruined
body of the good

man has been laid
under stone, & the stupid

thieves flung into
their places too—

A daylong hush:
nothing to be done

—only
the pathos of questions

skittering here & there
like jittery insects:

will the stem climb out of the bulb,
the sparrow out of the egg?

Sun in Fog

Bright white everywhere,
on the deck and in the garden

and even bits and pieces
on the floor—

shards of light afloat
in pools of shadow,

and on their edges faces that blanked
and vanished years ago,

jostling to be seen
in a blur that haloes

the grass, the tattered yellows,
the cloud across the sea.

Then suddenly it burns away,
the blue leaks back,

sears ghosts to nowhere, leaving
only the same plain

stranded day.

SAID THE SCRIBE:

in the highest high of whirlwinds,
way beyond the spinning dust devils,
Yahweh clenched His starry fist,

His beard flashed, His brows met in a line of fire:
You must never corrupt My Name, he muttered,
if a single letter should be deformed

bury My Word in the desert
as if you were laying to rest the dead
body of a beloved.

And so it happened, said the scribe,
that someone's brush slipped, the sacred ink splattered,
the Name was crippled by error,

and with due solemnity His worshippers
buried the Word among all the other
hides and clots of corruption—

                        and the shifting
sands passed over, glistening, and Yahweh
sulked in His tent of cloud

honing His intransigent will,
while down in the desert
where His Word lay O so deep

in a grave of clay,
a hundred godlings
rose from the filth of death,

and danced like young palms,
like a sweet oasis.

V.

LEI SOUP

The Same Ground

Think. How every day it's the same
& not the same, the weeds
the same & different,

& the same, same blades
& buds, same churn
of green, & the sea

likewise
sinks into its trough
of darkness & just the same

comes back from nowhere
all the same in the spin
& glitter where a single

feather
springs from my pillow
but all the same

I rest on this green linen
& turn my head
& see how you help me

for there you are this morning
not the same but
just the same

for now.

Seeds

Now they embark, bleak
travelers on a blurry track

that winds uphill in silence,
and they're blind, as if folded in fleece,

going forward and on and up,
no chance to turn back or see or stop—

and all around them the stillness thickens,
toughens, darkens

(and the passage so steep, so hard)
but shove—and step—and push—ahead

they go, they go on—and on
they come through black and brown

and films of gray
until the piercing through,

until the opening, the widening plain,
the shock of sky, the furnace of green.

The Zugspitze/Pike's Peak

In Garmisch-Partenkirchen
the Alps lumbered above us:
we looked up, around—
and saw
the looming of the Nazi peaks,

hateful transcendence, icy
hierarchy:
   Valhalla
winking in the distance,
the "material life" urging itself

up and out, bitter
matter, into
a spiritual sky,
    like Pike's
Peak, where the miners thought

the river currents
filtered gold, filtered
power from the mountain
mud and twelve tribes
worshiped the yearning

stones in
the garden of the gods.
On the Zugspitze, our skis
toppled us, our ankles
buckled, and we sat

laughing, chagrined, among intricate
walls of snow:
                        above us a massif
like the cry of Wotan when he shrieked
for Freya, the spirit of spring,

to come toward him, with her delicate
steps, along the ice-crust, among
the trembling aspens,
bringing the pure gold
bulb of the sun

over the Zugspitze and across Pike's Peak.

PARASAILOR

—FOR KAREN GALE

1.

Fiesta siesta on the breezy beach,
and up the purple parasailor goes,
over the smoke-green huddled hills—and watch!—
into the heave of the wind that sighs and blows
and over the shine of roofs, the glitter of sea
forever unfolding its lines of lights and darks,
its hiss of foam that the sailor's now too high
to hear as her silk umbrella turns and arcs
and dips into emptiness and rises to nothing
other than sky and sky—and look, look now,
how tiny the festal figures, how timid their bathing
just at the edge of the scrolled-out silk below!—
 so she wonders, regarding the knotty loops of the town,
 why can't she stay up here? why go back down?

2.

The bounce of clouds among the Mary blues
through which they swirl—and *she* swirls in a joy
of tip and curve, as if into a maze
invisible to most, though maybe Dante
once in mythic time had charted it:
this line's the crossing place where space and blank
meet light, and here in this silent dizzy spot,
is sunrise glow to eat and dusk to drink,
or so she imagines, swaying slower *here*
as suddenly fat blatherings and squawks
invade her little ecstasy of air—
a cruise ship like a worm that honks and talks!—
    its human sound a howl that reaches her,
      and tugs her back to the weight that beaches her.

SEAL VIEWING POINT: DISTURBANCE OF
SEA MAMMALS IS A FEDERAL OFFENSE

Sweet is the meadow, and sweet
for a walker from Queens, New York,
the breath of its juicy grasses,

green from California winter rain,
though the low tide beach,
its blanket of glimmering blue drawn back

reeks of the life and death
of weeds and other salty stuff we never
saw in my concrete playground,

and the fat white mounds of the beached seals
don't squeal like the brakes of trucks or bark
like leashed puppies——:

they twitch and lurch and bellow
at wild pools we never knew
and nakedly *disturb*

with tossing snouts
we couldn't have imagined
as we hopped and twisted

through the fenced-in
schoolyard or stood on
tiptoe at the zoo.

Mother and Child

In the seal colony
at the edge of infinite water
(though finite fish)
the mamas are barking orders
at their blobby babies,

rearing, flap-flippering
& now & then
turning their teats toward
air—sun—hunger
(are they indifferent?).

The rubbery baby
tubes of fishy flesh
squiggle around
like slick embellishments,
like variations on the theme of mama.

A few flop away from the huddle
toward the water where
everything is easier but nothing
is safe.
        One hangs clueless

in a black pool by the rocks
and the undertow slithers

around him, hooks him, starts its long
drag outward.
                    Does he

know what's happening?
Does his mama know?

Flocks

—FOR AARON DAVID GILBERT-O'NEIL

A huddle of fuzzy rocks cropping the field,
these nuzzling mothers live to eat a salad
of prickle, bristle & stalk; in warm or wild
air, they moon & baa as in the ballad.
Our two-year-old princeling points & bleats a mimic
bleat, & shrieks. He can't believe they're real!
They munch, they stare, they aren't in a book!
(They're busy as grown-ups, serious, & careful—)
& a hundred feet below, on the churning beach,
other stories are spinning strangely to life.
There's a faraway glitter his flung-out arms can't reach,
& an endless sound like a giant huff & puff,
& hurrying things leap up & rise & fall,
bringing him heap after heap of shining wool!

THE BERKELEY RAT

Think *scuttle*, think *soot*,
think shovel-shaped upside-
down mound of

yearning:
        black hump
of pubic bush

raging to raid & rape
the floor, the counter,
the cosy home of culture—

oh, that dangling banana!
ah, that naked peach!—
the fruit we stole from the old

decaying garden
where tiny incisors
sharpened into scalpels,

where a nose, tremulous & fierce,
learned to guide a desperate
gut into tunnels

past decorative ivy,
                    up & through
smug stone of the foundation,

& up again & again
through helplessly rusting
pipes into the lit

kitchen of transformation
                    & then,
after a furtive meditative wait,

past intricate spaces around the stove
into the night
where no love prevails.

The Paris Mouse

hunched over the greasy
burner on the stove
was *noir*, as in

film noir, as in
cauchemar,
as in *la nuit*

not *blanche* but
noire, the dream you can't
wake up from, meaning she

was a mouse *fatale*,
licking the old oil
glued to the old

cooktop, feasting
in her tiny hunched-up
sewer life

on fats & proteins for her
bébés all atremble in their
rotting *poubelle* nest,

so when I screamed my piercing
Anglo-Imperial scream of
horror & betrayal—

not *my* stove, not *my* traces of
pot-au-feu—
she leaped, balletic, over

the sink, the fridge, the *lave-vaisselle,*
& back to the *cave* & the trash she
scuttled, grim as a witch

in La Fontaine
who has to learn
the lesson we

all must learn:
Reality is always sterner
than pleasures of the nighttime burner

He's

blind in the blaze of
noon, animal Samson?

No, the mountain lion doesn't
have a Miltonic cell in his body:

his two-hundred-square-mile
hunting ground is his by

muscle & tooth, though in his
blurry daytime he

gropes through grasses,
sees your cat as a goat!

Be glad he's "shy
& elusive," wary behind

brambles so you don't even
glimpse him though he's

there, & huge, but not quite
sure what you are. . . .

If he does cast a clear
eye on you, say,

at dusk, when his pupils
widen & glow & his hunger rises,

put your tot on your shoulder
stand tall, don't run,

don't show him your back,
stay out in the open & O

if you must go into the woods,
never wear tan

(he might think you're a deer),
instead, says one online expert,

wear black & white,
(so he might take you

for a book,
        perhaps even

something Miltonic
& inedible).

For Ruth Stone on Her Ninetieth Birthday

Walter left but he didn't leave you alone.
Always there at the ragged edge of sight,
he left you a gift as tough and cold as stone.

You were young, you were wild, you beat at the sky and its rain,
you tore at the noose of bone, the stubborn weight.
Walter left but he wouldn't leave you alone.

You waded "grief—whole pools," like Dickinson.
You shrieked with laughter at the plots of fate.
In your battered jacket you traveled across the stone,

chopped ice from the brook, hung swirling words from your line,
simmered a broth for your girls in the flare of light:
Walter left but he didn't leave them alone.

And the words grew wilder and wiser and looped and shone
as you rode on "desperate buses" from state to state,
away from the past that dragged behind like a stone

until you reached a fierce house of your own
where you dwell in the light your sentences create.
Walter left but he couldn't leave you alone:
your gift of tongues made flesh and blood of stone.

Fourteen Fourteeners for
Sophia at 14 Months

Your first year, little one, to test the sweet & tawny grass
that tosses high above the sea in shifting bursts of light,
your first adventure on the gnarly ground that loops ahead!

Shiny pieces of black & orange flutter where you pass.
Attendant friends? Strange messengers? They rise & wait & float
as if they want to signal you without a single sound.

And look!—below us something blue that has to churn & hiss,
and over it, in lines now wiggling, now clear & straight,
come shrieking specks whose cries (like yours) ask to be
    understood.

Let's go slowly toward the noises, my fingers tight on yours.
Let's—or anyway let me—believe that you won't forget
this early trek into the radiant unlikely field.

Let's both remember, little one, the way you sallied forth—
your tiny swaggering stagger along the cliffside path.

Anti-Valentine

There wasn't any heart in the space provided.
In fact, *there's really nothing there,* said Cupid.
The nothing whirred and shimmered. *Try to slide it
shut,* he said, *it's just too fat and stupid.*

The lovers posed for souvenir photographs
with nothing squeezed between them, waving, winking.
Swarms of teens collected autographs.
Parades of weddings kept on honking, honking.

But out in the park the hearts were rolling away
as fast and slick as a pack of giant marbles.
Down the hill they went, into the shady
piney spots, and flung themselves like pebbles

at the old idea of a beloved window—
one that might open, if just to say *O no!*

Canticle of the plums

the size of babies' knees
the size of tulip globes
the size of the heads of kittens
the size of goddess eyes

the color of midnight
the color of moisture
the color of melancholy
the color of the wine-dark sea

the shape of July
the shape of the elbows of perfection
the shape of dreaming swans
the shape of moons in another galaxy

& sweet as the fevers of Tahiti

& moist as the tongues of the imagination

there in the left ventricle of your heart
where I should have my place
they are heaped like the flesh of a naked woman
who has abandoned herself to the most
intimate caresses

CALLA LILY, SHAMELESS

hussy flaunting
yourself like that—
opening your satiny creamy bridal
skirts to show

a burning orange pistil
stiff with pollen!
Balenciaga-girl-Armani-boy-in-
one, stuck on the grassy

runway to nowhere—sea
noises, unchanging
swoop of heaven over
head!—& wouldn't you

like to fly away with the
birds & bees that
visit you, especially the humming one
that zooms & whirs & stabs

the whole chill hole of you
again & again,
rending your satin & exploding
your shining tongue

with hungers you can't understand—

Hearing Aids

Hugging

When I put my ear next to his—
first one then the other—

our ears begin to sing together:
on the one side, a pure soprano

ascending to a Handelian high;
on the other, well,

maybe a young mezzo,
just embarking on

an erotic "Habanera."

Sex Sounds

Midnight. The usual intermittent shrieking
of cats & other animals—

& the young couple downstairs
just came in with a bump, a bang, & then

their voices slowly circling each other,
circling & deepening.

Outside pinecones drop with soft
voluptuous smashes into the garden,

& in a small wind, the petals of the plum tree
rustle open to show their stamens.

My beloved puts his head on my breast,
one ear next to my right nipple.

The whistle of his hearing aid rises,
delicate & sweet as mythic piping.

"Oh boy," he says aloud in his sleep,
with a certain satisfaction.

Later

he wakes to pull that
music from his ears

(& there's a tiny shriek
as if a small soul

leaped up, wondering,
what now?—):

                    then
the silence falls over

me too—
night blanket, night

heaviness, night in which
we speak to each other

mutely, as some
animals do.

Morning:

when I put my lenses in
the world returns to the spectacle it was
before darkness swallowed us.

We are visible bodies again!—

& now, with the chime
of an ethereal xylophone
(as if the music of the spheres

floated briefly toward us)
my lover's hearing aid
slides back into his ear:

we are speaking bodies too!

What does he hear

When those little buds of sound
are set in place:
                    a furry flurry

haloing each phrase?
& words of anger grizzling
as if dipped in tar & bark?

& when I'm earnest
a tiresome hiphopping
up & down a muzzy scale?

& if the children screech
a *how are you where are you*
eking & shimmer chiming?

& when at last
exhausted by whithers
& thithers of noise

he tears them out,
what then?
a glum puddle of

stillness or a
mystical
diapason?

     —FOR A.M.

Lei Soup

—because the orchids will only stay fresh in the fridge
for just so long & then their purple of curling
tongues about to kiss your neck will edge
to the black of a bruised fruit, spoiling . . .

—because the petals that look like perky bows
on junior high school girls or ribbons you won
at camp a lifetime ago will shred & lose
their shape & their satin will also be gone . . .

—because you want to keep the honey of color
& relish the scent that rises the first time you wear it . . .

you lift the whole bright garland from your shoulder
& dump it into your vat *& tear it & stir it*—

& can it or freeze it—the recipe isn't sure—

but maybe you'll drink your own lei soup, come winter.

Knowing

you
have

this hand	and this one
is good	is better
pull open	turn
the drawer	the page
hand	hand
take out	take up
the knife	the pen
the tool	

and look eyes
at what you
must see
and
beat
as you must
body be glad
of what you
can do
no drifting
girlishly
toward death
go on and
on grow old
as you must
old
woman

and lift this foot
and take this step   and the one
after